The Farm on the Hill

Jenn Best

BookLeaf Publishing

India | USA | UK

Presentation by *BookLeaf Publishing*

Web: www.bookleafpub.com

E-mail: info@bookleafpub.com

ISBN: 9789357448383

First edition 2022

DEDICATION

Dedicated to my family and my loved ones.

PREFACE

Morning sun along the cedars,
Hues of gold and auburn display;
Green and blue creek below it,
The beloved Loch-An Brae.

BEGINNINGS OF SPRING

Temperatures are rising,
The beginnings of Spring,
The ground is slowly softening,
Birds start to sing;
And there among the underbrush,
Lies a meditative buzzing.

Animals awakening
From Winter's rigid state,
Feel a familiar yearning,
They must attract a mate!
There is excitement everywhere,
In the warming of the climate.

In the highest rafters of the barn
The swallows build their nests,
They whistle tunes so hopeful,
They pray for good fortune at its best;
Working with such vigor,
They rarely break to rest.

As the days begin to lengthen,

And all spirits are soaring high,
I smile in wake of Spring's beauty,
I smile in rays of its sunshine;
I thank the Winter for passing,
For letting Springtime finally arrive.

THE SUN AND THE MOON

The sun as a star
      Knows not its existence,
Yet it is Creator
      Of all of life's presence

The sun as pure flame,
      Whose distance is not near,
Calls forth living things
      Throughout its solar year

Bright light that is heavenly -
      A beautiful magic thing!
Shines deep in all souls;
      It makes the birds want to sing

Cattle roll in grass,
      Life smiles in favour,
Life begins to soar;
      Souls bathe-in and savour

Trees stretch to limits,
      Of heights not yet reached;

To get to it closer
        And consume its warm heat

Light that shines brightly,
        To all those who bear it;
Its light shines both nightly,
        On the moon we can see it

Dark, holey craters,
        Its surface grey and blue;
The moon is our brother,
        From one we were made two

The moon as our other,
        Whose craters stretch vast,
Orbits monthly around us,
        Present becoming Past

The sun as a God
        Lying far beyond us;
It is Creator -
        Of life that is conscious.

BLUE SKIES

Upon the ground
I have found,
endless love
for blue skies
abound.

AN OAK TREE

There once was an old oak tree
Who stood both proud and tall;
On top a little green hill,
He was adored by all.

The farmers were all in awe -
The true greatness of its size!
Whistling tunes of adornment,
They could not believe their eyes.

All the critters loved the tree
And every day they would visit;
Climbing up its branches,
On strong, big limbs to sit.

The birds would often fly
To the highest branches of all;
So they could see the farthest
And hear their flock's call.

The deer all loved to lay
At its base so big and strong;
Within the grass around the tree,
In breaths of coming dawn.

The squirrels would gather acorns
That the oak tree often shed;
In Autumn when times get colder,
And critters start to make their beds.

But of all the animals there was
Only one that mattered most -
It was the raven's song,
Atop the tree, it made its post.

THE LAND

The forests are enchanting,
    With curtains of deep green light;
With every step that is taken,
    Wooded stillness comes alive.

Leaves begin to rustle,
    As I walk between birch trees;
Whispering prayers to myself,
    While treading fallen leaves.

In this land there is a power
    It is honest and it is true -
Its air is of another
    Energized by vast blue

Skies above it,
    A kingdom heaven all around;
I feel a magic energy,
    I can hear it in the sound

Of birds singing so joyously,
    In the sunshine that rains down,
It makes heaven feel so close;
    It makes the leaves on the ground

Look as though God is smiling,
    Colourful foliage all around.

RAVENS

They came one cold spring
After winter had just left;
We thought they were only crows,
Atop the silo they made their nest.

They would survey from its top,
Perched high above all else;
This was their new territory,
Their own worldly pedestal.

Only two there were to start,
And together they would roam
The fields and land around them -
What would now be called their home.

The ravens became quite curious
Of the farmers and their machines;
Who were plowing acres of land,
Planting large crops of hay and soybeans.

The farmers would always see them,
They could feel their dark cold stares;
From high up on above them,
When they looked, the ravens were always there.

The farmers and the ravens
Lived and worked the land as brothers;
They began to respect each other,
While protecting the land together.

When the snowy winter finally came,
The farmers figured they would leave at last;
But the ravens returned come springtime,
Building a nest for younglings to hatch.

THE BEES

Between two marigolds
The bumblebees dance,
With pollen on their feet
For all of nature's plants.

They make honey daily
In honeycombs of wax,
Golden sticky goodness
Filled right to the max.

They work every day
It's really all they know;
Helping the ecosystem prosper,
Letting diversity overflow.

Plant to plant they go,
A wonderful sight to see!
They are nature's little worker,
The striped, bumbling honey bee!

A GARDEN POEM

Basil, thyme
And everything fine

A bumblebee hums
In rain or shine

A ladybug crawls
across the grass

A blue jay sings
A song to pass

The time is all
But forgotten

Starlings murmur
In flocks a dozen

I work the soil
Pick rock and till

Rosemary, sage
Oregano and dill

Let there be rain
And warm sunlight

Heat, rain, and shine -
Three ingredients for life.

IN THE HEAT OF SUMMER (A haiku)

Sun rays beaming down.
Daylight in its resplendence;
LIFE in its glory.

BARN CAT SQUAD

The barn cat squad
Know just where to go,
If they find their food bowls are vacant;

To the farmhouse they trot
To let the farmers know
They need food, it's rather quite blatant.

"Just wait one minute,"
I grab my shoes and hat,
They meow with so much insistence!

To the barn we all walk,
Every cat in stride,
They are moving with so much persistence.

Orange ones,
Long-haired ones,
And tabby cats too;

There's blonde ones,
Grey striped ones,

And ones with white boots!

The barn door is barely open
Before they've all rushed inside,
Fierce determination they hold;

Pleased I have obliged,
And put food in their bowls,
They purr with bellies that are full.

THE FARM ON
THE HILL

For four long generations
Farmers of Scottish descent,
Have worked long, hard hours;
Full lifetimes have been spent.

Doing chores inside the barn,
Keeping cattle fed and healthy;
Tilling fields when weather is good,
Making sure bellies don't go empty.

The cows have been well bred,
Consistent, tall and straight;
The respect and admiration from peers
Has been gratifying and great.

A very rewarding lifestyle,
There are really no regrets -
When all things are considered
It's about as good as it gets.

LOVER

My lover, my dearest friend,
> It is hard to find the words;
You matter above all else -
> To me, you are the world.

Where my heart once beat heavily,
> You have loosened its weight;
You have shown me love when I had nothing,
> You have made time want to wait.

You have shown me only kindness
> Whenever life has brought me pain;
Given a hand for me to hold,
> You have been the light within the rain.

In shadows of black darkness
> Where sorrow once did lay,
You have shown how to love me
> And made my nighttime, day.

You fill my life with laughter,
> A new adventure every day;
To live several good years together,
> I am hopeful we just may.

MALVA SYLVESTRIS ZEBRINA

Malva Zebrina,
        My most favourite flower!
Shining ever so bright,
        Up high she does tower.

Her stem stretches tall,
        Leaves flat like dinner plates,
She blooms for many months;
        Buds tend not to wait.

She enjoys the cool shade,
        Where sunlight cannot burn;
She stands tall and fierce
        Until Winter takes its turn.

And when the cold comes,
        She lays down seed and waits;
Seedlings appear in spring,
        New life she creates.

Among a garden of perennials,
    Her beauty does overpower;
Malva Sylvestris Zebrina -
    My most beloved flower.

AUTUMN'S SORROW

The beetle's hum,
A rhythmic drum,
In the waning of the day;

A tree frog's song
Grows loud and strong,
While unloading wagons of hay.

Life seems so gay!
Then, to my dismay,
A gunshot clouds the day.

All the animals run
At sounds of steel guns,
To find shelter they must stay safe;

I see one fall,
A lone goose, quite small,
A death scene on display.

I know of no other
Sound that makes me shudder,

Than guns, whose shots go BANG.

To watch an animal fall,
With no good reason to it all,
I hang my head in such shame.

OCTOBER LEAVES

With every passing day
Many leaves turn red,
Another leaf turns orange,
Cold months lie ahead.

Displays of brilliant gold
In fallen leaves upon the ground;
Deep within my soul
I find peace in the sound,

Of birds singing tunes
In scales of B minor,
I whistle one back,
As a constant reminder;

Though the warmth wanes,
And creatures feel the signs,
Coming darkness does not scare us -
We embrace it with Autumn's shine.

THE HERD

Cows graze in pastures,
　　　　Grass glistens in morning dew;
Basking in pure delight of
　　　　The red clover newly bloomed.

Such curious beasts they are,
　　　　When people stop to say hi;
They stick their noses through the fences,
　　　　Greeting all who pass by.

The kids all love to giggle
　　　　At the feeling of their snouts;
They laugh when they get licked,
　　　　By their big slobbery mouths!

These beasts know only love,
　　　　Tales of abuse are often wrong;
They are respected by their farmers,
　　　　The bond they have is very strong.

The cows look so peaceful,
　　　　With plenty of space to roam;
Often seeming so grateful,
　　　　To call this heavenly place their home.

WINTER IS COMING

Fresh crisp air and Autumn leaves,
Signal another Summer's demise.

Predicting of the coming cold,
Deciduous trees turn shades of gold.

Plants blooming their last few flowers,
A final enjoyment of sunshine's long hours.

The ground grows cool and stiffens to touch,
I have never missed Spring quite this much.

Early mornings lay in hazes of frost,
The green of Summer's grass will soon be lost.

Daylight is shortening with every passing day,
To be cold and in darkness is Winter's old way.

BY THE FIRESIDE'S LIGHT

Bright fireside light,
Twinkling so bright,
Please keep me warm
On this cold, dark night.

Flame of such might,
Such a beautiful sight!
I find tranquil bliss
In throws of your light.

Red, yellow, white -
Colours that delight!
I feel your embrace,
My soul you ignite.

Solace in your being,
While animals lay sleeping;
In the still of the night,
Bright fireside light.

www.ingramcontent.com/pod-product-compliance
Lightning Source LLC
Chambersburg PA
CBHW070727160726
48003CB00006BA/2403